EX LIBRAS

This journal is dedicated to
Mrs. Mary Akers,
the Fifth Grade Teacher
who always said I would.

It's True... Our success depends on you!

Please take a moment to leave feedback on our Amazon page.

ISBN-13: 978-1493698660

And THANK YOU for your purchase!

The illustrations are by M.L. Baldwin.
Blue Icon Studio, Lexington, Virginia.

is a registered trademark of Blue Icon Studio

Most of us end up
with no more
than five or six
people who
remember us.
Teachers have
thousands of
people who
remember them
for the rest of
their lives.
-Andy Rooney

In a completely rational society, the best of us would be teachers and the rest of us would have to settle for something else.

Lee Iacocca

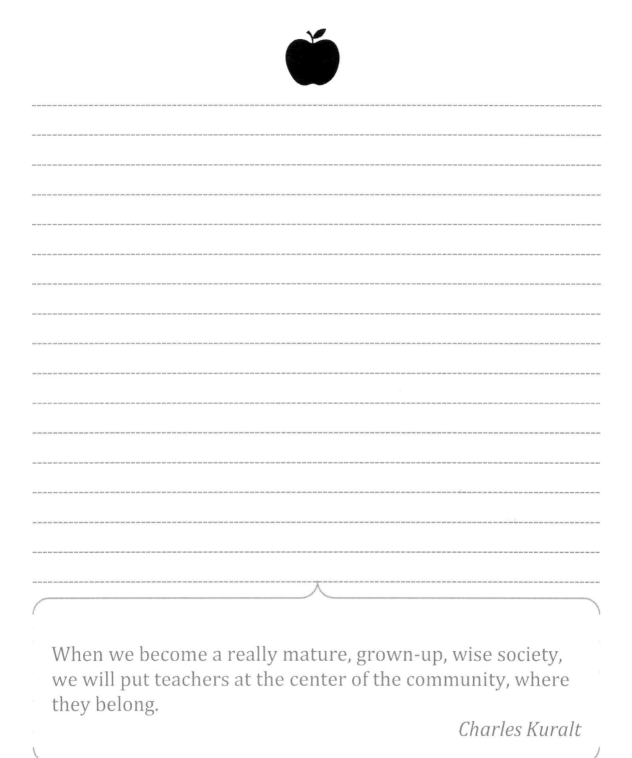

When we become a really mature, grown-up, wise society, we will put teachers at the center of the community, where they belong.

Charles Kuralt

Education is the key to success in life, and teachers make a lasting impact in the lives of their students.
Solomon Ortiz

Teachers can change
lives with just the
right mix of chalk
and challenges.
Joyce Meyer

I had many teachers that were great, positive role models and taught me to be a good person and stand up and be a good man. A lot of the principals they taught me still affect how I act sometimes and it is 30 years later.

Kevin James

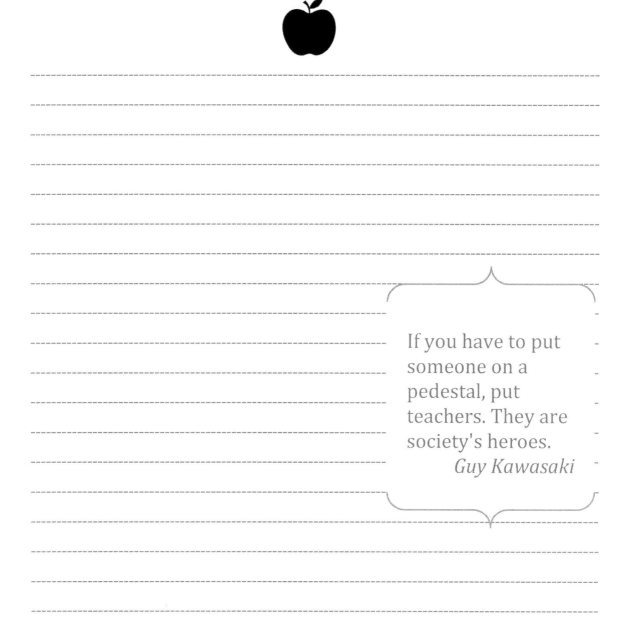

If you have to put someone on a pedestal, put teachers. They are society's heroes.

Guy Kawasaki

That is the difference between good teachers and great teachers: good teachers make the best of a pupil's means; great teachers foresee a pupil's ends.

Maria Callas

Everyone who
remembers his own
education
remembers teachers,
not methods and
techniques. The
teacher is the heart
of the educational
system.
Sidney Hook

Teachers started recognizing me and praising me for being smart in science and that made me want to be even smarter in science!

Steve Wozniak

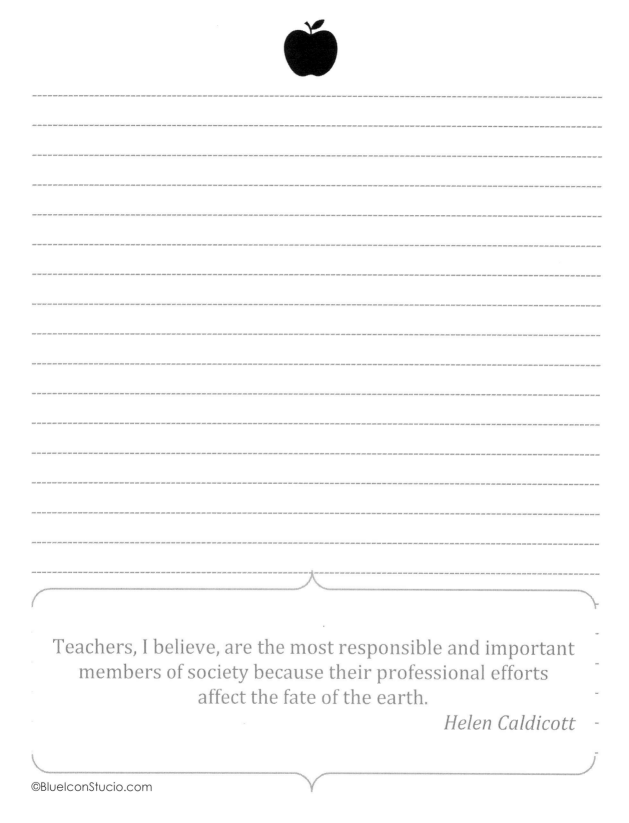

Teachers, I believe, are the most responsible and important members of society because their professional efforts affect the fate of the earth.

Helen Caldicott

Teachers teach
because they care.
Teaching young
people is what they
do best. It requires
long hours, patience,
and care.
Horace Mann

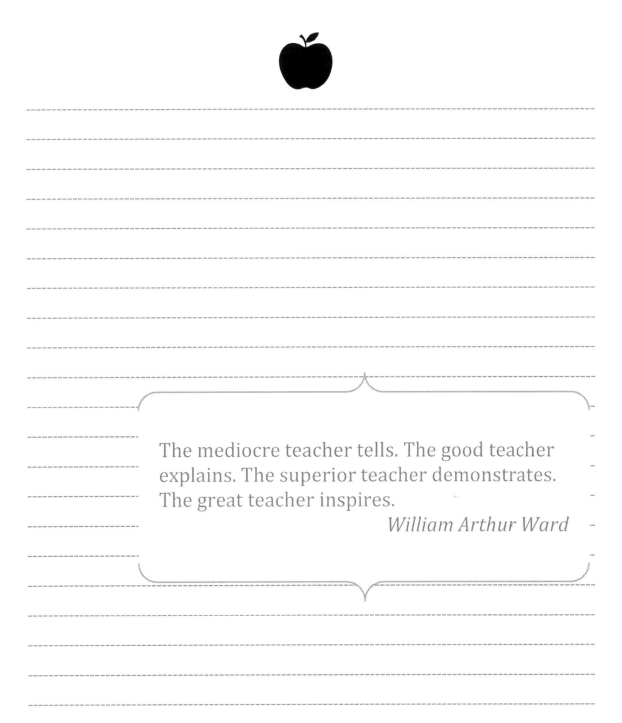

The mediocre teacher tells. The good teacher explains. The superior teacher demonstrates. The great teacher inspires.

William Arthur Ward

While I'm not a celebrity, it's such a weird concept that society has cooked up for us. Astronauts and teachers are much more amazing than actors.

Joseph Gordon-Levitt

Teachers are not
glorified babysitters
with summers off.
Their profession
fuels all others, and
on a normal day that
is amazing enough in
and of itself.
LZ Granderson

The art of teaching is the art of assisting discovery.
Mark Van Doren

If you plan for a year, plant a seed. If for ten years, plant a tree. If for a hundred years, teach the people. When you sow a seed once, you will reap a single harvest. When you teach the people, you will reap a hundred harvests.
Kuan Chung

Better than a
thousand days of
diligent study is
one day with a
great teacher.
Japanese proverb

The whole art of
teaching is only
the art of
awakening the
natural curiosity of
young minds for
the purpose of
satisfying it
afterwards.
Anatole France

Anyone who stops
learning is old,
whether at twenty
or eighty. Anyone
who keeps
learning stays
young.
Henry Ford

One looks back with appreciation to the brilliant teachers, but with gratitude to those who touched our human feelings. The curriculum is so much necessary raw material, but warmth is the vital element for the growing plant and for the soul of the child.

Carl Jung

Education is light, lack
of it darkness.
Russian proverb

Whoever first coined the
phrase 'you're the wind
beneath my wings' most
assuredly was reflecting on
the sublime influence
of a very special teacher.
Frank Trujillo

Treat people as if
they were what
they ought to be
and you help them
become what they
are capable of
becoming.

Goethe

Optimism is the faith that leads to achievement; nothing can be done without hope and confidence.

Helen Keller

Learning is finding out what
we already know. Doing is
demonstrating that you
know it. Teaching is
reminding others that they
know just as well as you.
You are all learners, doers,
and teachers.

Richard Bach

A hundred years from now,
it will not matter what kind
of car I drove, what kind of
house I lived in, how much
money I had in the
bank...but the world may be
a better place because I
made a difference
in the life of a child.
Forest Witcraft

Tell me and I forget. Teach me and I remember. Involve me and I learn.
Benjamin Franklin

It is not what is poured
into a student that counts
but what is planted.
Linda Conway

It is the supreme art of the teacher to awaken joy in creative expression and knowledge.

Albert Einstein

If a child is to keep alive his inborn sense of wonder, he needs the companionship of at least one adult who can share it, rediscovering with him the joy, the excitement, and the mystery of the world we live in.

Rachel Carlson

Education is not the filling of a pail but the lighting of a fire.
William Butler Yeats

Don't limit yourself. Many people limit themselves to what they think they can do. You can go as far as your mind lets you. What you believe, you can achieve.
Mary Kay Ash

The greatest sign of a success for a teacher...is to be able to say, "The children are now working as if I did not exist."
Maria Montessori

You have not lived
until you have
done something
for someone who
can never repay
you.
Anonymous

The purpose of life is not to be happy – but to matter, to be productive, to be useful, to have it make some difference that you have lived at all.

Leo Rosten

If you think
education is
expensive, try
ignorance.
Derek Bok

The whole purpose of education is to turn mirrors into windows.

Sydney J. Harris

Do not go where the path may lead, go
instead where there is no path and
leave a trail.
Ralph Waldo Emerson

Promise me you'll always remember:
You're braver than you believe,
and stronger than you seem,
and smarter than you think.
Christopher Robin to Pooh

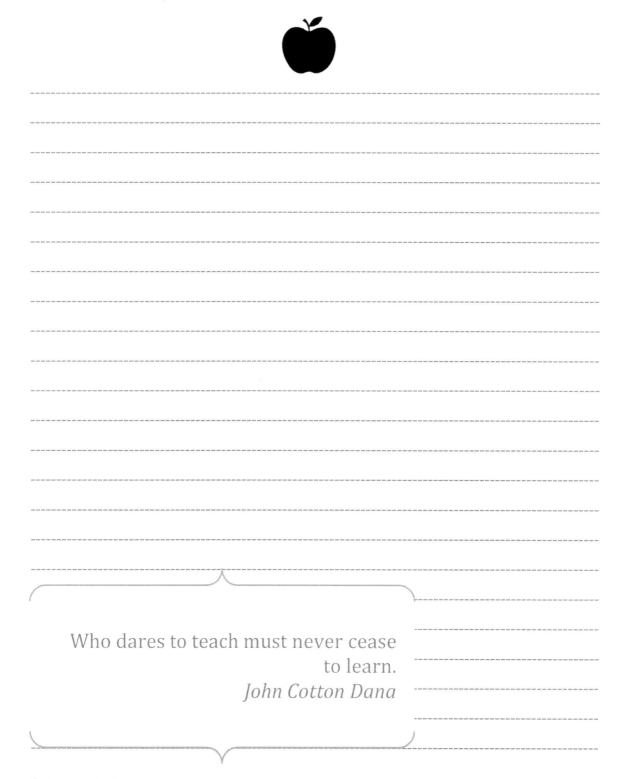

Who dares to teach must never cease
to learn.
John Cotton Dana

Everybody is a genius. But if you judge a
fish by its ability to climb a tree it will
live its whole life believing that it is
stupid.

Albert Einstein

I learned that a long walk and calm conversation are an incredible combination if you want to build a bridge.
Seth Godin

In the race of excellence there is no finish line.
H. H. Sheikh Mohammed bin Rashid Al Maktoum

Though no one can go back and make a brand new start,
anyone can start from now and make a brand new ending.

Anonymous

The more that you read, the more things that you will know.
The more that you learn, the more places you'll go.

Dr. Seuss

One person can make a difference,
and everyone should try.

John F. Kennedy

The true meaning of life is to plant trees under whose shade you do not expect to sit.
Nelson Henderson

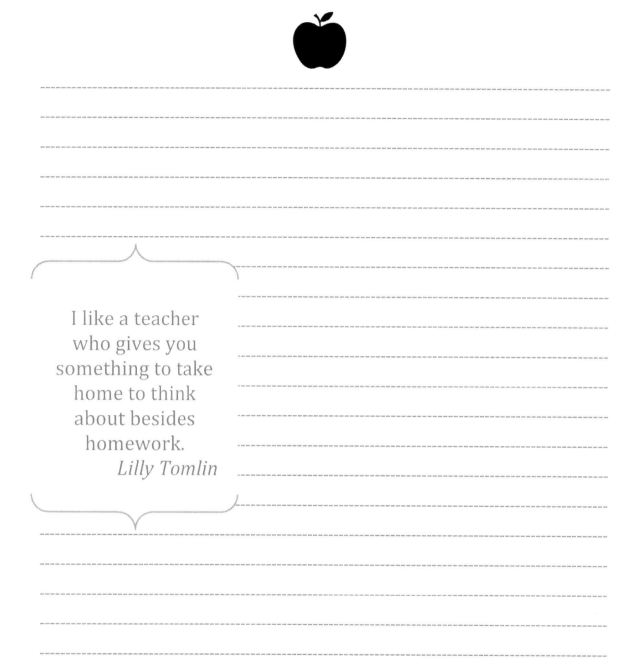

I like a teacher
who gives you
something to take
home to think
about besides
homework.
Lilly Tomlin

I cannot teach anybody anything,
I can only make them think.
Socrates

Any teacher that can be replaced
by a computer, should be.
David Thornburg

Change your thoughts and you
change the world.
Norman Vincent Pace

To know the rules
of the game, you
have to be
educated.
LL Cool J

Made in the USA
San Bernardino, CA
09 April 2014